THE
SALTILLO
SARAPE

1. Lennert, *Los Rancheros* (1830), Julio Michaud y Thomas, lithograph.

THE SALTILLO SARAPE

an exhibition organized by

THE SANTA BARBARA MUSEUM OF ART

catalogue text by:

JAMES JETER
PAULA MARIE JUELKE

photography by

MICHAEL CADEN

published by

NEW WORLD ARTS

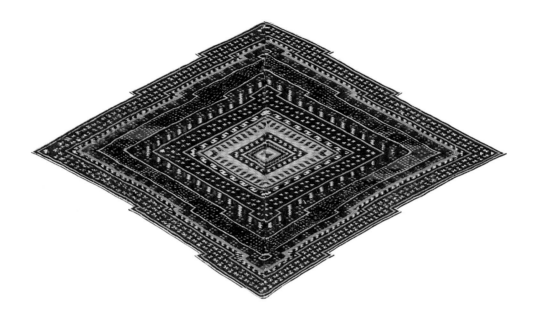

Cover: Saltillo Sarape, Catalogue No. I

Library of Congress No.: LC78-60702

Copyright: June, 1978
        New World Arts
        1520 Willina Lane
        Santa Barbara, California 93108

Catalogue designed by Richard Kubiak

Acknowledgements

Probably less than three hundred classic Saltillo sarapes are still in existence. Very few have survived intact, although some are in surprisingly good condition. There are approximately 150 known examples in various museum collections scattered throughout the United States. The balance (an estimated figure) are those Saltillos in private collections and in foreign museum holdings. The private collector and art dealer have long been instrumental in the acquisition, preservation and interpretation of art. Anson W. Hard, Fred Harvey and William Randolph Hearst were such collectors. The intelligent and farsighted efforts of these and other individuals have formed the few museum collections of Saltillo sarapes.

Today, as then, the private collector is invaluable in assembling these magnificent textiles. Only through the assistance of the following people has the creation of the New World Art Collection of Saltillos been possible: Messrs. Bob Ward, Jack Cassin, Stan Pepper, Mike Haskell, Fred Jimenez, Fred King, Chris Selser and Tom Buffalo. We would also like to express our appreciation for the generosity of Mr. Michael Caden, Mr. John Gale, Mr. David Hall, Mr. Peter Brock, Wizard and Rose, and the Santa Barbara Museum of Natural History for lending examples from their Saltillo collections.

We wish to thank the Santa Barbara Museum of Art for the support and enthusiasm which made this exhibition possible.

Our deepest appreciation is extended to Dr. Carl S. Dentzel of the Southwest Museum for his personal interest in this project and for making available to us pictorial references of the Saltillo sarape.

The photography was ably handled by Michael Caden, in conjunction with Image Makers Studio of Santa Barbara and Leven Jester of Palos Verdes.

The professional expertise of Richard Kubiak, both in the production of the catalogue and in arranging the exhibition itinerary, is gratefully acknowledged. Mr. Terrell Hillebrand, Director of Education and Curator of Collections for the Sarah Campbell Blaffer Foundation of Houston, Texas, deserves our thanks for his encouragement from the very inception of this project and for his efforts in encouraging the Santa Barbara Museum of Art to undertake the sponsorship of this exhibition.

A special debt is owed to Katharine D. Jenkins, Dr. Joe Ben Wheat, and Joanne Segal Brandford for their substantial contributions to research and the understanding of the history of the Saltillo sarape. Their willingness to share information and to exchange ideas is deeply appreciated.

Finally, we would like to acknowledge Mrs. Hope Jeter, Mrs. Sue De Mayo, Mrs. Connie Caden, Mrs. Lisa Jeter, and Josephine and F. M. Juelke for their support and interest in seeing this project come to a successful conclusion. Above all thanks to L. Ron Hubbard, through whose technology dreams come true.

Jim Jeter   Santa Barbara
Paula Marie Juelke   May, 1978

2. Julio Michaud y Thomas, *Gente del Pueblo* (detail), 1830s, lithograph.

Salute the Saltillo Sarape

With the great revival of interest in native American arts it is only natural that attention would be focused on the uniquely beautiful Saltillo sarapes of Northern Mexico. Contemporary artists and craftsmen are studying native techniques of spinning, dyeing, and weaving to better understand the textile arts of aboriginal America and the developments relating to them. Inevitably, a greater appreciation will result as the creative techniques are better understood in relation to the remarkable heritage contemporary society has received from pre-Columbian America as well as the Spanish Colonial and Mexican periods of the American Southwest.

The so-called Saltillo sarape, a distinctive piece of wearing apparel, has deep roots in North America. In style, design, texture, and color it relates to the pre-Columbian inhabitants of Mesoamerica. As a garment it had a multiplicity of uses in the everyday and special occasions for the society that utilized it.

First, native American cotton, then later, after the Spanish conquest, wool was woven into a variety of clothing. Styles, shapes and designs were more or less traditional, utilizing patterns hundreds of years old. The woven garments reflected the ingenuity of aboriginal inhabitants as well as the society that conquered them. The subsequent result was a fascinating merging of cultures, arts, crafts, and particularly weaving techniques. There was an artistic and aesthetic evolution particularly in evidence in Northern Mexico and Southwest United States.

As a textile art form the Saltillo sarape was developed and utilized by the inhabitants of Northern and Western Mexico in the late 17th, 18th and 19th centuries, with a decline in the early 20th century. So distinctive were the products of the looms of Northern Mexico that many travelers commented on the weaving industry, particularly upon the beauty and the utility of the Saltillo sarape. Throughout its development the Saltillo sarape became a useful and prized possession as well as a sought-after collector's item.

Artists depicting life in Mexico in the 18th, 19th and 20th centuries often showed the utilitarian Saltillo sarape. Since that garment had so many uses it is revealed being utilized in all segments of Mexican society. Few items sketched or painted by artists could rival the color of the Saltillo sarape. Horsemen particularly were among its greatest users and admirers. They found this useful garment valuable in all aspects of horsemanship. Artists depict the *vaqueros,* the *caballeros,* and the *charros* wearing this colorful garment.

In Mexico's struggle for independence in the first quarter of the 19th century the Saltillo sarape style was often shown associated with the native American revolutionaries. It became a symbol of *Mexicanismo;* its influence was widespread, inspiring many copies.

Nineteenth century travelers in Mexico generally commented on this picturesque textile. Sailors from many countries visiting Mexico's ports purchased Saltillo sarapes as souvenirs of their adventuresome voyages.

In the course of the Mexican War, 1846-48, many North American soldiers passing through Saltillo and other Northern Mexican towns purchased sarapes as mementos of their tour of duty in Mexico. Grandmothers, mothers, aunts, sisters, sweethearts, and the parlor pianos were the beneficiaries of the soldier tourists from the North.

The Treaty of Guadalupe Hidalgo which marked the end of the Mexican War also seems to mark the end of the classic Saltillo era. It seems probable that the time-consuming artistry of the great Saltillo weaving was unable to survive the years of political and social unrest. It should be noted that it was the artistry of the classic era, and not the sarape industry, which was a victim of the War. Following the Mexican War, in response to an ever-increasing demand the industry continued to flourish.

Throughout the 19th century, artists from Spain, France, Germany, England, Austria, and the United States produced many beautiful publications with prints and lithographs of all aspects of life in picturesque Mexico. In those books showing life in the cities and country many of the plates depict Mexicans with their treasured Saltillo-styled sarapes.

As an item of use and trade, particularly in Northern and Western Mexico, the Saltillo sarape became an almost fabled textile for marketing. Throughout the American Southwest—Texas, New Mexico, Arizona, and California—the dazzlingly beautiful and useful textile was sought after. It was the object of many trading transactions throughout the 19th century. Its orbit included a good part of Mexico and Western North America.

The Western ports of Mexico, Manzanillo, San Blas, Mazatlan, and Guaymas were places where the Saltillo sarape was a tempting item of commerce. From those ports for many years the Saltillo sarape found admirers, traders, and collectors enough to make the sarape known in Hawaii, the Northwest Coast, the Philippines, Japan, and China.

With the annexation of the Mexican Northwest (which formed the American Southwest) to the United States after the Mexican War, native products lost popularity and fell into disuse as new commercial items appeared from the East. However, after 1860 native weaving, especially among the Pueblo and Navajo Indians, began to supplant some textiles that used to come in abundance from Northwest Mexico. Many of the woven Indian garments, blankets and rugs were influenced by the Mexican prototypes of fifty or a hundred years before. As population grew in the newly acquired lands along the border, Texans, New Mexicans, Arizonians and Californians slowly succumbed to the cheap, gaudy, manufactured textiles from the American East, Europe, India and the Orient.

Now, after more than a century, the people of the highly populated areas of the American West have begun to realize the artistic and aesthetic value of the distinctive folk arts of their region. They are reevaluating their precious heritage. One of the most inspiring aspects of that heritage is the rich legacy of weaving and the remarkable textiles produced by the Indians and the Mexicans for centuries.

So today aficionados of weaving around the world have stimulated collectors and others interested in unique creative crafts in rediscovering the Saltillo sarape. They recognize its unique position in the world of textiles. They appreciate its influence on many creative textile developments among the aboriginal inhabitants of the Mexican Northwest and the Southwest of the United States.

Today museums everywhere are endeavoring to interpret and show outstanding contributions of natives from all parts of the world. The rediscovery and recognition of the Saltillo sarape is long overdue. Through the efforts of James Jeter and the Santa Barbara Museum of Art attention is finally focusing on this long overlooked textile.

The Southwest Museum along with other museums across the country is pleased to participate in this revival. The founder of the Southwest Museum, Charles F. Lummis, was an early enthusiast of Native American Weaving, especially the Saltillo sarape. This exhibition is a tribute to the artistry, skills, and genius of the artisans of Northern Mexico.

CARL SCHAEFER DENTZEL
Southwest Museum
Los Angeles, California

3. James Walker, *California Vaqueros* (detail), 1870s, collection of Carl S. Dentzel

The Saltillo Sarape: History

Sometime during the colonial period of Spain's New World empire, textiles now known as Saltillo sarapes were woven in northern Mexico. In this arid territory, over 500 miles north of Mexico City, were produced wearing blankets of such exceptional beauty that their fame became truly international in scope.

The precise history of Saltillo sarapes is not known. Even the most basic information — origin of design elements, identities of artisans and owners, exact places and conditions of manufacture — remains subject to speculation. Although private journals, government reports, and general histories of the region mention these garments, very few of them include much detail, and often the data which can be gleaned from such sources are contradictory. In the succeeding pages, a brief summary of some of what is known about Saltillo sarapes is presented. Further facts about the origin, development, and eventual decline of these garments must await more extensive research into primary sources such as hacienda inventories, wills, dowries, and industrial and labor legislation of the colonial era.

The sarapes which are the central focus of this discussion are known by the generic term "Saltillo," after the town of Saltillo, in the present State of Coahuila (see map, p. 18). In actuality, not all of the sarapes were produced in Saltillo; rather, there were a number of weaving centers scattered throughout the mining communities, sprawling cattle and sheep ranches, and vast agricultural fields of northern Mexico. Because Saltillo was the most famous of these textile manufacturing towns, the term "Saltillo" gradually came to be associated with any finely-woven sarape of that time and region. Besides Saltillo, San Miguel de Allende (formerly San Miguel el Grande), Guanajuato, Querétaro, San Luis Potosí, Zacatecas, and other cities are among those mentioned as having produced sarapes of similar quality and design.

SOURCES OF DESIGN

Tracing the development of the Saltillo sarape is complicated at the very outset by controversy over the origin of the sarape itself. It is generally accepted that this type of wearing blanket was not indigenous to Mexico, but represents, as so many other Mexican arts do, a unique blend of native and Spanish elements.[1]

While the exact evolution of the sarape is far from explicit, the pattern of development of the sarape called Saltillo is somewhat clearer. In its classic form, the Saltillo sarape manifests certain design elements which help to explain its history.

The skillful use of colored yarns to achieve a mosaic effect may be singled out as the most obvious feature of these wearing blankets. Saltillos usually had three principal design fields: the outermost zone was a frame or border enclosing the second zone, a "background" field of different, and often simpler, design. A large central lozenge or circular medallion formed the third zone. While there were countless variations on these design themes, these three elements are recognizable in all sarapes called Saltillos. Occasionally, the sarape had a neck-slit (*bocamanga*) permitting it to be worn as a poncho.[2] The central design then formed a colorful yoke around the wearer's shoulders.

Each of the principal design zones was made up of myriad smaller motifs, such as triangles, hourglasses, lozenges, ovals, and rhomboids which were used in various combinations to achieve multi-hued patterns that often seem to vibrate because of the sharp angles of the designs and the sudden shifts in color. Brilliance of color and the frequent use of stripes in Saltillos undoubtedly prompted the native Nahuatl name for these sarapes: *acocema-lotic-tilmatli*, "rainbow mantle."

Archaeological finds in northern Mexico offer some potential clues to the development of the Saltillo design system. Dry caves discovered in the State of Chihuahua have yielded cotton textile fragments, dyed with indigo, which have strikingly similar patterns.[3] In particular, the serrated and concentric diamonds are distinctly reminiscent of Saltillo lozenges. There appears to be little evidence of European contact associated with these finds. The designs on the textile fragments suggest an indigenous, rather than a foreign, origin.

Equally promising are archaeological remains uncovered in another dry cave, La Candelaria, only 150 miles northwest of the city of Saltillo (see map, p. 18). Originally discovered in 1953, this particular site, which included several burials, yielded a rich array of pre-Columbian weaving, as well as an assortment of other artifacts. Although the material recovered is of relatively late date (c. 1000-1600 A.D.), the find is especially valuable since it provides an idea of the type of weaving skills employed in this region on the eve of Spanish contact.

Assembled as they are in different combinations, many of the design elements appearing in later Saltillo sarapes are present already in these prehistoric fragments. While some of the patterns found in these early examples of weaving were probably incorporated into Saltillos, it is likely that their chief source of inspiration came from an entirely different direction, several hundred miles to the south. In 1518, when Cortés first launched his invasion of the New World, one of the first native groups he encountered was the Tlaxcalan nation, subject to the Aztec empire. The Tlaxcalans put up a stiff resistance to the invading Spaniards but, after they were conquered by them, they allied themselves with the Spanish cause in an effort to free themselves from their Aztec overlords. Because of their assistance in the assault on the Aztec capital of Tenochtitlán (the present-day Mexico City) and their unflagging support throughout the wars of conquest, the Tlaxcalans were granted several privileges, including exemption from paying tribute to the Spanish king. Along with Spanish privileges, however, came Spanish institutions. One of these which had a lasting impact on Tlaxcalan life was the Spanish woolen textile industry.

Very little is known about any indigenous Tlaxcalan textiles, except that they certainly had a tradition of weaving in cotton and other vegetal fibers using the kind of backstrap loom found throughout Mesoamerica. The production of woolen goods necessitated some major changes in approach, but also built on existing technology.

By the end of the 16th century, the Spanish-introduced woolen industry in Tlaxcala was thriving. A large estate at Apizaco, a few miles northeast of Tlaxcala, typifies the organization of these self-sufficient communities. Besides the textile shop itself, there were two mills in operation—one for fulling the finished cloth, and the other for grinding grain for food. Sheep for wool and cattle for meat were grazed on adjoining pastures. The owner's and workers' dwellings completed the compound.[4]

In addition to their direct role in the weaving industry, the Tlaxcalans were also called upon to provide critical assistance in the colonizing of northern Mexico. With the discovery of rich silver lodes in the region of Zacatecas in the mid-16th century, the whole northern frontier became the focus of new settlement. This northward push, however, was not without its difficulties. The native populations, referred to collectively by both Spaniards and Tlaxcalans as "Chichimecas" (loosely translated as "dirty low-down dogs"), were fierce fighters and elusive raiders. Entire decades of warfare did not succeed in containing or pacifying the local Indians. The policy which eventually proved to be most fruitful was one of a less bellicose nature. A sustained program of clothing and food distribution, together with the importation of pacified, Hispanicized Indians as colonizers, finally brought some measure of peace to the north.

In 1591, four hundred Tlaxcalan families were recruited to help settle the northern frontier. It was hoped that, by their example, the Chichimecas would learn "plowing, sowing, and harvesting, their management of animals, their building of houses, their weaving and domestic arts, their churchgoing, and their monogamous family life."[5] In August of the same year, eighty of the families making the northward trek arrived in Saltillo. They selected a nearby site for their own settlement, which was named San Esteban de Nueva Tlaxcala. This community was separate from both Spanish and native Indian dwellings; the Tlaxcalans had stipulated this arrangement in their original agreement before leaving Old Tlaxcala.

So successful were the colonizing efforts of the Tlaxcalans that they were often called upon to help settle newer areas even farther north. Tlaxcalans soon were playing a major part in this pacification process. In fact, the name "Tlaxcalan" came to be applied, throughout the colonial period, to any of the Indian settlers so employed, despite their actual heritage.

The early arrival of the Tlaxcalans and their already well-established weaving technology in the region of Saltillo make it very plausible that the Saltillo sarape could have been developed by them. European-style looms probably accompanied the Tlaxcalan immigrants to their new home in 1591.[6] Certainly the technical complexity of Saltillo sarapes argues for an early date for their inception. The Tlaxcalans probably borrowed from the design vocabulary of textiles woven by indigenous, sedentary Chichimecas who had been resettled near Saltillo. This explanation could partly account for the Saltillo sarape's origin in the north, rather than near Old Tlaxcala in the south.[7]

Other possible sources of influence on the Saltillo design system were Oriental and European fabrics which found their way in great quantity into the northern provinces. Spanish garments, of course, provided one of the first exposures to a new array of design motifs. The volume and assortment of textiles which were sent north from Mexico City exceeded all other exports to that region. A typical shipment, loaded on wagons and pack trains, might have included coarse woolen cloth and blankets in a variety of colors, cotton blankets, cloth from China and Holland, Spanish shirts, capes, cloaks, and skirts.

The importation of Chinese silks and East Indian cotton fabrics began shortly after the Spanish conquered the Philippine Islands in 1565. For 250 years, until 1815, the Manila Galleons plied their annual circuit to Acapulco and back, transporting literally tons of Far Eastern merchandise. Ready buyers were waiting in Mexico when the galleons arrived. So marked was the predilection for Oriental goods that most of the imported cargo was purchased in Mexico, very little surviving the transcontinental haul to Veracruz where it was reshipped for export to Spain.

Despite the number of imported textiles, however, it is doubtful that the Saltillo sarapes owe very many of their design elements to foreign inspiration. Neither the Moorish-derived patterns from Spain nor Chinese motifs offer very precise parallels. Under such circumstances, the nearly contemporaneous fragments of textiles from the northern caves seem far more reasonable as models. One possible exception is the elaborate circular medallion, ascribed to Oriental influence, which replaced the diamond center in many Saltillo sarapes. The exact configuration of influences and derivations will probably never be known, dependent as it must have been on the personal taste, experiences, and weaving abilities of so many individuals.

It is almost futile to hope to discover a series of datable textiles stretching from pre-Columbian times down to the Saltillo which would illuminate the pattern of their development. Unlike Peru, whose cold, dry climate has preserved such an astonishingly complete record of pre-Hispanic weaving, much of Mexico is subject to high humidity and heavy rainfall. Political and social turmoil throughout Mexico have also taken their toll on luxury items such as Saltillo sarapes. For this reason, finds such as La Candelaria achieve even greater significance. There are few regions in which climatic conditions (and mortuary customs, in this particular case) are favorable for the preservation of pre-Hispanic textiles.

WEAVING AND DYEING

Curiously, many extant Saltillo sarapes are in surprisingly good condition, having retained both the suppleness and integrity of the cloth and the vibrancy of the dyes. It is known that Saltillos were always greatly treasured and that they commanded high prices from the very beginning. For these reasons, it seems that special care must have been exercised in storing them, and perhaps even in wearing them. It is likely that they were the sort of possession which was cherished and handed down to succeeding generations through marriage portions and through bequests, or which changed hands in business transactions such as transfers of hacienda ownership.

In an examination of the Saltillo sarapes which have survived the passage of time, certain consistencies of structure, as well as design, are noticeable. The classic Saltillo sarape was woven in a weft-faced tapestry weave; that is, plain over-and-under weaving in which the weft yarns are so tightly packed together that the warp yarns are no longer visible. To separate zones of color, the weavers of Saltillos utilized a technique known as *kelim*, which results in tiny slits in the fabric where the weft yarns double back on themselves instead of continuing across to the next warp yarn. In cases where the weft and warp counts are particularly high and where the designs are based on acute angles (as in Saltillos), these slits are neither very large nor apparent.

The materials used to weave Saltillo sarapes were fairly limited. Wefts were almost always wool, although later examples made some use of cotton and, to a lesser extent, metallic yarns. Warps were either cotton or linen. Occasionally warp yarns were dyed with indigo, but most were undyed, natural, off-white fiber. Both weft and warp were characteristically very finely and tightly spun.

Merino wool was probably used in the weaving of Saltillos, although undoubtedly only after being subjected to a thorough scouring, as it is particularly oily and can resist absorbing dyes unless properly cleaned. Another trait of this type of wool is its distinct, tight crimp. Although merino wool is not an especially long-stapled fleece, it does have the advantage of compacting during spinning to yield an extremely fine, thread-like yarn, a definite asset in executing intricate designs. In order to maximize this potential, the wool may have been carded against a wooden board using only a single brush (rather than by the more common method of using two brushes pulling in opposite directions with the fibers in between). When one carding comb is used, the hank of fleece is braced against the board with one hand and brushed straight out with the other, in the manner of brushing hair. This method ensures that the fibers all lie in the same direction, resulting in thinner yarn.

The colors so characteristic of the Saltillo style were obtained from a variety of natural dyes, the most prominent being cochineal (*grana*) and indigo (*añil*). By the time harsher aniline dyes were introduced into Mexico, during the last quarter of the 19th century, the era of the classic Saltillo was over.

Cochineal is derived from the dried bodies of females of a parasitic insect (*Dactylopius coccus*) which infests the prickly pear cactus (*nopal*, or *tuna*). Approximately 70,000 insects are needed to make a single pound of cochineal, which is sufficient to dye only two pounds of wool. Depending on the type of mordant used, cochineal yields shades of red which vary from purple to orange, but the most characteristic has a distinct bluish tinge.

Cochineal was a dyestuff well known to the Indians of pre-Cortesian Mexico. Bernal Díaz del Castillo, a soldier who accompanied Cortés, reported that great quantities of cochineal were offered for sale beneath the arcade in the marketplace of Tenochtitlán.[8] As early as 1525, only four years after the fall of the Aztec capital, Spaniards began to cultivate cochineal for export to

Spain. Eventually, cochineal was second only to silver in export importance.

Because of its great value as a trade commodity, the raising and harvesting of cochineal was supervised by the viceregal government. One of the richest cochineal-bearing regions was the territory of the Chichimecas, especially the area around San Luis Potosí, halfway between Saltillo and Mexico City. Cochineal plantations were also encouraged in the south, Old Tlaxcala being one of the most important centers of production. By the mid-16th century, the Tlaxcalans, "observing the heavy profits to be derived from cochineal . . . developed skillful techniques of deceit. Native sellers deceived Spanish buyers by adulterating the product with pitch, sand, or ground stone, and selling such mixtures as pure cochineal."[9] To prevent such abuses, Viceroy Martín Enriquez (1568-1580) established the office of *juez de grana,* or "cochineal judge." In addition to inspecting crops and regulating prices in accordance with government standards, he determined to which of four grades the harvested produce should be assigned: *grana fina, granilla, polvo de grana,* or *grana silvestre.*[10]

Indigo was also an aboriginal dye plant used by the Indians, but the Spaniards apparently regarded the native product as either of inferior quality or insufficient for their own needs, for they imported indigo and established plantations in Mexico during the mid-16th century. Although it never achieved the economic significance of cochineal in terms of a cash crop for export to Spain, cultivation of indigo played a prominent role in Mexico's social history, requiring thousands of laborers, including both Indian and black slaves.

Indigo produces a clear, long-lasting blue-violet. Compressed cakes of pure indigo were much in demand in Europe, where it replaced woad, a vegetal dye yielding a duller, murkier blue.

In addition to the predominant colors red and blue, Saltillo sarapes also reveal limited amounts of yellow, green, and purple. Yellow dyes were obtained from plant sources which included, according to a traveler in Mexico in the 1820's, *sacatlascal,* an extract from the seeds of a parasitic plant, and *palo morelete,* derived from a tree growing in the hotter regions of Mexico. Purples and greens were produced either by admixtures of cochineal and indigo, and indigo and a yellow dyestuff, or from other vegetal sources.

Browns and blacks are colors which occur in natural wool, but the weavers of Saltillo sarapes do not seem to have made much use of undyed yarns, with the exception of natural off-white wool, found in almost every example. Rich golden-browns were probably obtained from Brazilwood, and "Campeche wood" (logwood) probably produced the deep, pure blacks for which Mexican textiles, especially silks, were noted. The Renaissance Spaniard's decided preference for somber, black clothing may partly explain the shipments of logwood sent from Mexico to Spain.

The exact origin and nature of dyes used in Saltillo sarapes are, in most instances, impossible to ascertain without chemical analysis of the yarns, but distinctions between earlier, natural dyes and later, harsher, aniline hues are readily perceptible.

Wool was most likely dyed before spinning to insure a more evenly color-saturated yarn. European spinning wheels had been introduced into

Mexico early in the 16th century, but they probably were not used in making yarns for Saltillo sarapes. Hand-spinning produces a much stronger, thinner thread than the treadle-driven wheel. Warp threads, which had to withstand a great amount of tension during the weaving process, were probably hand-spun, even when weft yarns were not.

Saltillo sarapes were woven on European horizontal frame looms. Most of these looms were quite narrow, accommodating textiles of about two feet in width. As a result, the majority of sarapes were woven in two separate strips and seamed together. The skill required to duplicate the intricate pattern on each panel so that the designs of the two halves, when joined, matched and appeared as a unified whole is clearly phenomenal. Some sarapes were woven in a single, wide panel; those with medallion centers seem to fall into this category rather regularly.

In weaving sections where color changes were not frequent, as in end stripes, the sarape-maker employed a large shuttle (*lanzadera*), throwing it back and forth across the full width of the loom for the number of weft rows needed. In weaving less extensive sections, where various colored yarns were needed in rapid succession in a single weft row, smaller shuttles or bobbins (*canillas*) were used. The weaver passed the bobbin beneath as many warp strands at a time as the design required, lifting them with his fingers. Far from being a simple mechanical process, the weaving of Saltillo sarapes, with their myriad and sudden shifts of color, clearly must have been accomplished by laborious hand work. It has been estimated that, in order to duplicate a Saltillo sarape, a master weaver would have to labor ten hours a day for eight consecutive months.[11] The loom served primarily to keep an even tension on the warp threads and to hold the finished product. In many respects, despite their cumbersome appearance, the large upright looms were not much different from the traditional backstrap loom, on which complicated patterns were laid in with the fingers. Later sarapes, with their preponderance of wide horizontal stripes, took advantage of the mechanical efficiency of the horizontal loom, but at the expense of technical virtuosity and aesthetic effect.

Weavers of early Saltillo sarapes, in order to maintain uniformity in design, may have made use of some type of pattern or guide. Modern backstrap weavers often refer to fragments of older garments—or even to the clothes they are wearing, if they still use their traditional dress—in order to check on the motifs or the layout of a particular pattern. While it is highly unlikely that "extra" Saltillo sarapes would have remained long enough in workshops to serve as models, it is quite possible that a painted diagram might have supplied the same requirements. Such an arrangement could explain the amazing similarity between some pairs of sarapes. A report submitted to the Viceroy in 1793 may allude to such a pattern board. It relates that in San Miguel de Allende wool blankets were woven "over tables painted with the same."[12] Much later, in a Zacatecas workshop in 1925, sarape weavers placed portraits whose likenesses they were working into sarapes below the warps, copying the image free-hand. The observer who noted this also commented that the weavers undoubtedly made use of a grid in order to count the stitches, but that it was not apparent from the finished product.[13]

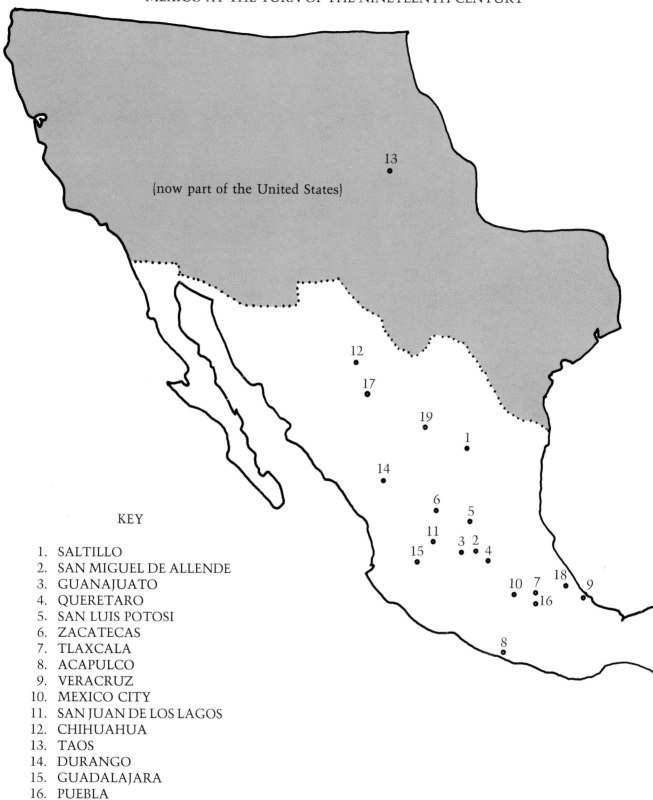

(now part of the United States)

KEY

1. SALTILLO
2. SAN MIGUEL DE ALLENDE
3. GUANAJUATO
4. QUERETARO
5. SAN LUIS POTOSI
6. ZACATECAS
7. TLAXCALA
8. ACAPULCO
9. VERACRUZ
10. MEXICO CITY
11. SAN JUAN DE LOS LAGOS
12. CHIHUAHUA
13. TAOS
14. DURANGO
15. GUADALAJARA
16. PUEBLA
17. PARRAL
18. JALAPA (XALAPA)
19. CANDELARIA CAVE
. . . .MODERN MEXICO — U.S. BORDER

THE WEAVING INDUSTRY IN MEXICO

The identity of individual *saraperos*, or sarape weavers, is rarely known, although the beauty of the garments they wove attests to their mastery of the art of weaving. To arrive at a reasonable idea of who they might have been, it is necessary to understand how the production of sarapes belongs to the larger pattern of development of the Mexican textile industry. Two entirely different systems of weaving technology met and merged with the arrival of Spaniards in the New World. Inasmuch as a highly-productive indigenous industry already existed, the Spanish system can be regarded as a mere overlay. But in at least two respects, the introduction of wool and the dependence on male weavers, profound changes were made.

In pre-Hispanic times, cotton and *ixtle* were the principal textile fibers in Mexico. Cotton, a native plant, was of some antiquity: carbon-dated remains from caves near Puebla yield dates of approximately 5800 B.C. By 5000 B.C., cotton was a cultivated crop. *Ixtle* is derived from the fibrous leaves of the maguey, or agave, plant. Although *ixtle* is a strong, serviceable fiber, the smoothness and sheerness of cotton made it much more esteemed for use in clothing. As a result, cotton garments were worn by native priests and nobility, while commoners had to content themselves with clothes of *ixtle*.

Weaving, spinning, and embroidery were all performed by women in pre-Cortesian Mexico. Some individuals achieved such a high level of proficiency that they were regarded as a separate class or group of professionals. These women wove especially detailed patterns, such as those which decorated the borders of garments. Luxury materials—including feathers, wild silk, and dyed rabbit hair yarn—were frequently employed in these design zones.

The advent of sheep to the New World followed hard on the heels of the Spanish Conquest. The first breed to be introduced was that known as "churro," primarily valued for meat rather than their coarse wool. Soon after, flocks of merino sheep were imported from Spain at the instigation of either Cortés, himself, or the first viceroy of New Spain, Antonio de Mendoza (1535-1550), who wished to improve the quality of his own herds. By the end of the 16th century, huge herds of sheep were not uncommon. Although the flocks were pastured throughout the plateau regions, the largest flocks were concentrated around Mexico City, Puebla, and Tlaxcala, and northward around the mining communities of San Juan del Rio and Querétaro. The pattern of raising sheep near textile mills, as at the Tlaxcalan estate of Apizaco, was fairly common by the end of the 16th century. Among the most prosperous hacienda operators, in this regard, were the Jesuit communities. In the 17th century, flocks belonging to the Jesuits were estimated to number in the hundreds of thousands. Most of the wool was not exported to Spain, but sold through domestic markets. While some percentage of the fabric produced in Jesuit-operated textile factories supplied their own clothing needs and those of their hacienda workers, it is likely that a sizeable profit was still realized from this type of enterprise.

Vast flocks of sheep posed a serious problem for agriculture, however. The unfenced animals grazed through pasture and planted field alike. When the Chichimeca territories opened for settlement, many herds, including those of Viceroy Mendoza, were driven north to take advantage of the expansive open ranges and excellent pasturage.

Besides the introduction of sheep and wool weaving, the Spaniards created, in effect, a new type of artisan: the male Indian weaver. It probably never occurred to the Spaniards to teach native women weavers the use of the mechanical loom. Like so many other conquering peoples, they imposed their own way of doing things on the conquered. Sixteenth-century textile production in Spain was a highly structured, guild-controlled industry in which men were occupationally classified as shearers, wool cleaners, combers, dyers, spinners, warpers, weavers, and fullers. Occasionally, women were employed as spinners, but it was essentially a male-dominated mode of production. As a result, the Spanish-influenced textile industry in Mexico also reflected this same division of labor. Women continued to weave on backstrap looms, producing native garments for home consumption, and to spin strong cotton yarns needed to warp the European looms on which the men wove. The success of this new industry was immense and immediate. Within the space of only fifty years, looms in southern Mexico could duplicate the quality of any woolen goods produced in Spain.

Despite the importance of *obrajes* in Mexico's textile economy,[14] by the 18th century a shift in emphasis toward smaller workshops was taking place. At the same time, an increase in population was creating a larger pool of free laborers—far less expensive than slaves and far less troublesome than prisoners. Many slaves were freed by their owners once it became financially unfeasible to maintain them. It has been estimated that in 1793 there were no more than 10,000 slaves in New Spain.[15] The small weaving workshops operated by free workers, rather than the *obrajes*, were responsible for the growth of the weaving economy in Mexico. San Miguel de Allende, for example, though renowned at the time for its fine sarapes, was described as having only 318 looms in 1802. No more than four *obrajes* were ever in operation there.[16]

One feature of this extensive cottage industry was what is known in England as the "putting-out system." Basically, the system involved the distribution of wool by the textile shop owners to Indians living in nearby communities. The wool, delivered on credit, was spun into yarn and returned to the shops, where it was worked up into cloth. Sometimes merchants acted as middlemen between Indians and shop owners, and sometimes they enacted the role of suppliers of raw materials and purchasers of finished products, bypassing the owners completely.

Judging from the scarcity of references to textile manufacturing in the northern provinces, smaller-scale production of woven goods must have been the rule there. In many respects, the entire northern region was completely different in nature from the southern provinces with their relative proximity to Mexico City and the viceregal government. The ruggedness of the terrain, the rough-and-ready atmosphere of the mining communities and the incontrovertible remoteness from the capital city resulted in a distinctive character not unlike that of the West in the United States.

While divisions between social classes were rather rigid in the south, they tended to be blurred or obliterated by the exigencies of frontier life.

The northern Indians, especially those in the mining communities, seem to have benefited from this more liberal climate. They became wage-earners on the ranches and in the mines, or worked in their own businesses as craftsmen and shopkeepers. Adopting the Spanish language, dress, and horsemanship, they often constituted a moderately well-to-do class. At least some of these independent Indian merchants and artisans were probably involved in limited production of textiles.

Various sources attest to the almost total lack of a weaving industry in the north, even at the time when high-quality sarapes were supposedly being woven—from the mid-18th century to the mid-19th century.[17] San Miguel de Allende, San Luis Potosí, Aguascalientes and Zacatecas are among the towns singled out as sarape-manufacturing centers, but for which few statistics such as numbers of looms or weavers can be found to substantiate the claim. Even Saltillo, the most famous, and probably first, sarape-weaving city, presents puzzling contradictions in this regard. Ramos Arizpe, a government official writing in the early 19th century, deplored the underdeveloped state of the textile industry in Saltillo. In a formal report submitted in 1823 he complained that unprocessed cotton and wool had to be exported to factories in the south, and the finished products purchased at high prices, because they could not be manufactured locally. In the same report he mentions that there were approximately forty looms in Saltillo which wove only "coarse cloth," a description hardly applicable to Saltillo sarapes.[18]

What all indications seem to suggest, however, is that sarapes were woven on such a small scale that contemporaries did not regard them as products of an "industry." It seems likely that Saltillo sarapes were woven either in San Esteban de Nueva Tlaxcala, or in one- or two-loom shops on local haciendas, or in both of these places. Looms were certainly to be found in the Tlaxcalan community, and at least one source states positively that sarapes were made by master weavers working in shops on landed estates. The hacienda workshops must have been of a completely different character than the southern *obrajes*. It is impossible to reconcile the delicacy of Saltillo sarapes with the rude realities of the *obrajes* described so pungently by Humboldt. Literally sweatshops, they were far better suited to turning out yard after yard of coarse woolen cloth and the plain, rough-textured blankets called *fresadas*. Shops where sarapes were woven would have been much smaller and certainly much healthier establishments, where the abilities of the weavers (and the weavers themselves) were respected.

It is also possible that the Church or weaving guilds may have taken an active role in the manufacturing of sarapes. Finely woven sarapes were always extremely costly and represented a substantial investment. It is interesting that an inventory of items belonging to a New Mexican chapel in 1818 includes twenty sarapes.[19] It is at least possible that Mexican religious houses also occasionally stockpiled such luxury items which could be sold when needed. Considering the well-established connection between, for example, the Jesuits and textile mills, it is easy to imagine that a few master weavers might have been retained on sheep *estancias*.

Guilds, which controlled the textile industry in Spain, were also present in the New World. The first guild established in Mexico was that of embroiderers, in 1546. Basically, a guild was a group of artisans who enjoyed the exclusive right to engage in a particular profession. They were subject to various ordinances which they had promulgated and which had been sanctioned by the government. One critical aspect of guild organization was a rigid hierarchy based on class. Only Spaniards who could supply evidence of their *limpieza de sangre,* "purity of blood," could attain the rank of master. *Castas,* as those of mixed racial heritage were called, were relegated to the lower ranks of minor officers and apprentices. While all artisans supposedly belonged to a guild, and guilds existed for all types of crafts, it is unknown how much force these rules had in the more northerly regions. It is known, however, that the guild system was active throughout the 18th century in the area known as the Bajío, comprising Querétaro, Celaya, San Miguel de Allende, Guanajuato and Aguascalientes. During that century guilds came under the attack of two different segments of Bajío society. The businessmen sought to break the guild monopoly on production of goods, conducted by guild members in small shops. They hoped either to incorporate the shops into a larger system, or replace them altogether by factory methods of production. The *castas,* on the other hand, chafing under their frustrated hopes for advancement, sought to abolish at least the discriminatory requisite for becoming master artisans, if not the entire guild organization.

During the same century, the Spanish court at Madrid enacted a number of economic reforms in Mexico. These generally took the form of encouraging the production of raw materials—especially cotton, wool, flax, hemp and wild silk—while suppressing manufactured goods. Domestic manufacture was not entirely curtailed, however. The abundance of raw materials in Mexico and the high price of European and Asian merchandise produced a stimulus to Mexican industry that even Spain could not prevent. By the turn of the 19th century, four major—though gradual—changes had taken place within the Mexican colonial textile industry: First, free labor rather than forced or indebted labor characterized the work force; second, larger *obrajes* were steadily losing ground to smaller workshops, known as *trapiches,* which were often family owned and operated; third, control of the textile industry was passing into the hands of the Indians who, as laborers, had long been the foundation of the textile industry, but had only recently begun to acquire ownership of shops; and fourth, regional specialization in types of textiles manufactured was beginning to occur, based on the kinds of raw materials most readily at hand. Cotton textiles were produced primarily in the south, around Puebla, and woolen goods in the north, particularly in the Bajío region.

TRADE FAIRS

Commerce in Mexico, like industry, was greatly affected by policies generated in Madrid. Royal patronage of trade with the Orient placed Mexico squarely in the middle of a thriving international market. The so-called Manila Galleons sailed to and from the western port of Acapulco, and Spanish supply ships, leaving from Veracruz, returned to Spain laden with silver specie, cochineal, indigo and other dyestuffs, chocolate, coffee, tobacco, sugar, and other products of New Spain. A network of roads connected the two ports by way of Mexico City. In an effort to control this commerce as much as possible, the Spanish government, to the benefit of Mexico City merchants, decreed that Veracruz and Acapulco were the only ports through which international trade might be conducted.

The result of this monopoly was a system of trade fairs which diffused imported goods throughout Mexico. Since the fairs were held at different times of the year in different places, a regular route for fair-goers developed, with merchants leaving one fair and traveling toward another. Trade fairs established in the northern provinces were critical factors in the economic life of several towns, including Saltillo, San Juan de los Lagos, Chihuahua, and Taos, in New Mexico. Commerce in these far-flung regions was not limited to these annual fairs, but they did represent a major social, as well as financial, event. The mining roads leading from Chihuahua through Durango and Zacatecas and on to Guadalajara or Mexico City were well-traveled thoroughfares by the 17th century, though still subject to Indian raids and other marauders such as escaped slaves and convicts. Thousands of mules arrived in Mexico City every week bringing ingots of silver, hides, tallow, wine and flour. On their return they carried woolen cloth from Puebla and Querétaro, merchandise from Europe and the Philippine Islands, plus materials needed in the mines, such as iron, steel and mercury.

By the 17th century, a considerable trade had developed between the Spanish colonies in New Mexico and the mining districts to their south. In 1637 a merchant in Parral received 1,900 yards of *sayal* (coarse woolen cloth) and approximately 500 cotton *mantas* (cloaks), the latter of Pueblo Indian manufacture.[20] Less frequently traversed trade routes ran east and west from the Sinaloan and Sonoran coasts to the mining communities.

Most important of the northern trade fairs was that held every September and the first part of October in Saltillo. Originally founded in the mid-16th century as a defensive settlement against the Guachichiles, the local Indian population who formed part of the so-called Chichimeca tribes, Saltillo rapidly gained importance in economic as well as military respects. Part of its significance was due to its strategic location at a gap in the mountainous terrain of northeastern Mexico. Called *la llave de la tierra adentro*, "the key to the interior lands," Saltillo represented the commercial capital for much of the area incorporated by the modern States of Coahuila, Durango, Zacatecas, San Luis Potosí, Tamaulipas, and Nuevo León, in addition to Texas, known at the time as the "New Philippines." Even merchants from distant Sinaloa and Sonora made the trek east to attend the fair. Pack trains of mules bearing provisions for settlers, troops, and missionaries, and gift goods to help in the pacification of the Indians, were periodically dispatched from Saltillo. Items not sold in the Saltillo fair were also sent via these convoys to the Taos fair in northern New Mexico.

The Saltillo fair was established in the early 17th century and continued until the advent of the railroads delivered the death blow at the turn of the 20th century. Principal goods offered for sale were agricultural and livestock products from the local region. European and Asian merchandise was sent north to Saltillo after the fairs of Jalapa and Acapulco were over. Hundreds of fair-goers converged on Saltillo from all directions each year. Business was so bustling that the municipal government was obliged to construct barracks near the church and in the plazas to serve as temporary housing.

As a result of the great distance from the southern ports, and the profits extracted by all the intervening middlemen, prices of imported items were often scandalously high in Saltillo, and higher still as the merchandise traveled even farther inland. Besides the original cost, articles manufactured in Europe carried export duties from Spain, import duties from Veracruz, transportation costs, and excise taxes from each Mexican marketplace along the way.[21]

Although domestically produced, the Saltillo sarape was still one of the costliest commodities for sale at the Saltillo fair. As the fair drew to a close during the first part of October, merchants and professional gamblers frequently invested large sums in obtaining as many Saltillo sarapes as they could, later disposing of them at other trade fairs along the circuit and in Mexico City. This demand for fine sarapes apparently stimulated both increased output and elaboration of these garments.

The end of the colonial period was the beginning of the end of the classic Saltillo sarape. Political unrest in northern Mexico which began in the first decade of the 19th century and continued almost unabated for over a century had an adverse effect on commerce and industry. This period of unrest, and possibly the suppression of gambling at the Saltillo fair, contributed to the decline in the quality of Saltillo sarapes.[22] The Mexican War seems to mark the end of the classic Saltillo period and the beginning of the post-classic period.

INFLUENCE OF THE SALTILLO SARAPE

Saltillo sarapes, carried from the fair in all directions, made a lasting impression on a number of other textiles. The Saltillo style was incorporated into sarapes woven throughout Mexico and across the border far into the southwest United States. Modern derivatives of the Saltillo design system can even be discerned in the striped cotton blankets, dyed in strident aniline colors, offered for sale in curio shops from Oaxaca to Tijuana. There are four regions, however, where the impact of the Saltillo sarape made itself especially apparent: the traditional sarape-weaving centers of central Mexico; the Rio Grande Valley in northern New Mexico and southern Colorado; the Navajo territories; and the Mayo and Tarahumara lands of present-day Sinaloa, Sonora, and Chihuahua.

Although the beginnings of the tradition are not known exactly, the late 18th century marks the apogee in the weaving of Saltillo sarapes. During the same period, other textile manufacturing centers also produced sarapes which closely resembled the Saltillo style in both design arrangement and excellence of weave. Because of vagueness of contemporary 18th- and 19th-century descriptions of these garments and the general lack of sufficient collection data for extant examples, it is impossible to state with any degree of certainty which sarapes were woven in which places.

Most consistently mentioned as a rival of Saltillo was San Miguel de Allende, located some four hundred miles south of Saltillo in the State of Guanajuato. A number of sources assert that San Miguel sarapes actually surpassed Saltillo sarapes, but either because of the design's origin in that town or the pre-eminence of the fair, the name "Saltillo" was applied uniformly to all finely-woven sarapes of the same style.[23] A handful of possible diagnostic features can be gleaned from scattered references; however, none of them has been shown to be conclusive in distinguishing the products of the two towns: sarapes from San Miguel de Allende may have zones of narrow, parallel stripes at each end, woven in the predominant color of the rest of the textile; they may include those sarapes having scalloped, circular medallions in the center, either replacing or enclosing the more usual diamond motif;[24] and they may have utilized unraveled wool yarn in the weft.[25]

After about 1830 contemporary illustrations such as prints and paintings reveal Saltillo or Saltillo-style sarapes (see illustrations 1-4). Sarapes purchased at the Saltillo fair and traded or carried north undoubtedly account for a good many of the copies executed on colonial New Mexican looms. Duplication of Saltillo sarapes represented a substantial challenge which was not met by Rio Grande weavers, due to their inexperience with the intricate Saltillo patterns (plates XXVI, XXVII). Although increased familiarity brought about a marked improvement in technical expertise, the Rio Grande sarape never achieved the intricacy and fineness of the Saltillo.

Another possible source for the introduction of Saltillo motifs in Rio Grande sarapes concerns two brothers, Ygnacio and Juan Bazán, who were sent to Santa Fe, New Mexico as weaving instructors in 1807 on a six-year contract. By 1800, profits derived from exportation of New Mexican woven goods had fallen off to such an extent that officials in Mexico City made efforts to restore the sagging economy. The Ministers of Royal Hacienda and the Army were instructed to recruit weavers "of skill and good conduct and especially men free of vice and drunkenness" to go north as weaving consultants.[26] The precedent for importing master weavers had been established in the early 16th century when Archbishop Quiroga sent for European weavers to help increase and improve production of native goods in Michoacán.

The Bazán brothers arrived in Santa Fe with instructions to establish a cotton-weaving industry and to teach Rio Grande artisans better methods of spinning, dyeing and weaving.[27] Although there is no certain proof that these master weavers were responsible for the addition of Saltillo elements to the Rio Grande design vocabulary, the coincidence of their arrival, followed shortly by the appearance of Saltillo-style sarapes is extremely suggestive of a possible connection.

Some examples of Navajo weaving, notably the Sarape and Eye-dazzler styles, also show their kinship with Saltillo sarapes (Plates XXV, XXVII). The Navajos acquired the upright loom and certain decorative conventions, such as simple stripes on a broad horizontal field, from their more sedentary neighbors, the Pueblo Indians. From the Spanish settlers in the American Southwest, the Navajos adopted a new array of design elements, a vertical design format, and perhaps an emphasis on tapestry weave as well.[28] Sarape-style Navajo blankets probably date to the mid-19th century.[29] During part of this time, beginning in 1864, the Navajos were confined in captivity at Fort Sumner (also known as Bosque Redondo), where they experienced deprivation and hardship for four long years. At one point, in an attempt to ameliorate the situation, the United States Government authorized the delivery of 4,000 Rio Grande blankets to the captives. Of the 1,000 that actually arrived at the fort, the vast majority was probably of the simple striped or banded variety. A few, however, must have utilized more complex Saltillo design elements, such as concentric diamonds and serrated zigzags, for the Navajo women were soon incorporating them into their own weaving. By 1885, Saltillo designs had become dominant in Navajo blankets.[30] Probably the most striking example of the connection between the two was the Eye-dazzler style which reinterpreted the mosaic effect of Saltillo colors in the new medium of commercially-spun, aniline-dyed Germantown yarns, first introduced in 1875 (Plate XXVII).[31] While it is possible that actual Saltillo sarapes may have reached the Navajo, it is far more likely that the Navajo design system was most directly affected by the more prevalent Saltillo-derived Rio Grande textiles nearer at hand. It is interesting to note that the exchange of design elements between Rio Grande and Navajo weavers was mutual: Spanish-American artisans also wove imitations of the "Sarape Navajó," which sold for a considerable sum.[32]

Today, two northern Mexican Indian populations—the Mayo of coastal Sinaloa and Sonora, and the Tarahumara in Chihuahua—continue to weave heavy woolen blankets which have Saltillo-like patterns.[33] Mayo women, using native horizontal looms, produce both sarapes and *cobijas*, or blankets. The latter are intended for domestic use, primarily, and are generally coarser and plainer than the sarapes, which are usually made for sale. Some sarapes are also woven by men on mechanical looms like those used in colonial times. Mayo sarapes seldom contain dyed yarns, but still achieve a mosaic effect by careful manipulation of shades of natural wool colors. The use of small geometric motifs, such as hourglass figures, parallelograms, serrated diamonds, triangles, and spot repeats, and the general format of the design, which often includes a frame or border, all reflect their Saltillo heritage.

Inland from the Mayo territories, in the northern region of the Sierra Madre Occidental, the Tarahumara inhabit a rugged homeland where temperatures are often low and winds blow sharply. Woolen blankets, made by Tarahumara women on horizontal looms, are loosely woven to take full advantage of the wool's natural insulating properties. Like the Mayo, Tarahumara weavers primarily use undyed natural yarn; some commercial dyes and commercially dyed and spun yarns are employed in limited amounts, however. Concentric and serrated diamonds, zigzags, parallelograms and hourglass motifs are used as central figures and in horizontal bands.

Mayo and Tarahumara weavers may have received their inspiration directly from Saltillo sarapes which were traded west, or indirectly through contact with Rio Grande or Navajo textiles. In 1838, for example, over 21,000 Rio Grande blankets were sold in northern Mexico, adding significantly to the pool of Saltillo-influenced sarapes in general circulation.[34]

One rather curious and minor offshoot of the Saltillo family tree was the European printed version. Machine-made in Germany or Belgium sometime after 1880, they were intended as cheaper versions of the genuine article (Plate XXIX). A concomitant feature of mass-production, of course, was that many identical examples were turned out and marketed at the same time. A few Saltillo sarapes had apparently been exported to Europe since at least the early 18th century. They appear on cargo manifests along with cochineal, indigo, and other colonial agricultural products, as well as fabrics from Puebla, Tlaxcala, Querétaro, and San Luis Potosí.[35] Some of the more unusual sarapes to be sent were manufactured later, in the mid-19th century when the era of the classic Saltillo was over and innovations in design and materials had transformed the style.

Portraits of heads of state and other dignitaries were frequently woven into these "specialty" sarapes. One, which bore the likeness of Pope Pius IX in the center and the pontifical coat-of-arms in each corner, was sent to the Vatican in 1877. Other portrait or heraldic sarapes included those of George Washington with the flag of the United States (Plate XXX), and the Mexican national emblem of eagle and serpent. President McKinley was presented a sarape which bore the image of a tiger, and the Mexican General Porfirio Diaz, one with a view of the Castle of Chapultepec.

THE SARAPE AS SYMBOL

Among the materials woven into later sarapes were aniline-dyed yarns which added an entirely new palette of hues, silk, and gold and silver metallic threads. Variegated wool yarns were used to create subtle shadings of color in the main design field, perhaps as a substitute for the same effect formerly achieved by the dexterous manipulation of separate color zones. It is possible that the elaboration of sarapes was partly prompted by requests from merchants who frequented the fair and were accustomed to buying in large quantities. More probably it was the natural outcome of over a century of experimentation in meticulous weaving technique and sumptuous colors. One other factor, however, is undoubtedly significant in the increased opulence of sarapes during the 19th century—a growing sense of Mexican patriotism, especially after Mexican Independence in 1821, which adopted the sarape, a uniquely Mexican garment, as its symbol. The proliferation of sarapes with political themes, and even those decorated with pre-Columbian motifs, can be ascribed to this movement.

Closely allied with this nationalistic fervor were the aficionados of *charrería*, a brand of Mexican equestrianism which was virtually a cult of horsemanship. In the first decades after Conquest, Spaniards had enforced laws which prohibted anyone of non-European descent from riding a horse. As a result, horses quickly came to be associated with a privileged upper class. Even the word *"caballero"* incorporated both the ideas of "gentleman" and "horseman" in a single term, while the word for common laborer, *"peón,"* implied a "man on foot." Skill in riding was a prime requisite of the colonial Mexican gentleman and equestrian showmanship was an integral part of celebrations held by the aristocracy of New Spain.

With the opening of the mining districts and the establishment of huge sheep and cattle ranches, however, the prohibition against non-Spaniards riding horses was no longer practical. Indian, mestizo, black and mulatto vaqueros and muleteers logged thousands of miles in the saddle. Their skill in riding soon became prodigious and the Spanish hegemony over horsemanship was challenged and abolished. Before long, a hardy, independent, and highly mobile class of these horsemen had developed. Besides evolving new types of saddles, spurs, and other equipage which suited their special needs, they also gave rise to a distinctive mode of dress which included leather chaps, wide-brimmed hats, and sarapes. Perfectly suited for life on horseback, the sarape served as all-weather cloak, bedroll, and colorful saddle trapping. Those who could afford them bought the luxurious and highly-prized sarapes of Saltillo or San Miguel de Allende. Probably more than a few were won from the gamblers who invested in quality sarapes before leaving the Saltillo fair in October.

Throughout the Mexican Wars of Independence, the majority of those fighting for the insurgent cause was drawn from this self-sufficient class of horsemen. After the wars, the idealization of their mode of life spawned many of the *charrería* associations which have persisted to the present day in Mexico. The emphasis on superlative riding and roping abilities, showmanship, elaborate riding costumes, and all the accoutrements of equestrianism is the hallmark of Mexican *charrería*.

It is very likely that Saltillo and other sarapes have always been connected with the riding of horses. At first, elaborate sarapes were probably the exclusive property of the wealthy upper classes, just as the horse itself was. Gradually, however, the garment—because of its eminent suitability—was adopted by workers on haciendas and others whose labor caused them to spend long hours on horseback.

In its own time, the Saltillo sarape was widely acclaimed for the brilliance of its colors, harmony of design, and excellence of weave. A number of questions remain to be answered concerning the history of these colonial garments and the textiles which influenced them and were, in turn, influenced by them. It is hoped that the sarapes included in the present catalogue will lead not only to a fuller appreciation of a truly extraordinary example of the weaver's art, but to a better understanding of the processes affecting individual creativity and the nature of a changing art form in a particular social setting.

PAULA MARIE JUELKE

Notes

(Full citations for references will be found in the Bibliography)

1. Possible prototypes of the sarape include the *tilma*—the native cotton garment worn by men throughout the Aztec empire—a variety of Spanish cloaks, and the Peruvian *poncho*. While each of these garments has something to recommend it as an ancestral form, none is sufficiently like the sarape to have been the sole model.

2. Mena, p. 393; Marín de Paalen, p. 112. The Spanish name for a sarape-like garment with a neck opening is *jorongo*.

3. Mera, Plates I and II.

4. Gibson, p. 135.

5. *Ibid.*, p. 183.

6. An itemized list of shipments—including looms and carding instruments—sent from Mexico City to Zacatecas during the years 1590-1597 appears in Powell, *Miguel Caldera*, pp. 216-217.

7. The existence of these sedentary Chichimecas is discussed briefly in Johnson, pp. 5 and 8, and in greater detail in Aveleyra A de A., *passim*.

8. Díaz del Castillo, p. 233.

9. Gibson, pp. 149-150.

10. Heers, p. 7. The four categories are listed in descending order of quality.

11. Marín de Paalen, p. 113.

12. Florescano y Gil, p. 64.

13. Mena, p. 398.

14. The term *obraje* is used to describe the large southern textile shops or factories which were operated with slave and prisoner labor and which produced the inferior grades of woolen textiles. Humboldt's famous description (p. 189) of one of these *obrajes* is a fitting indictment of a cruel system.

15. Wolf, p. 191.

16. Brading, pp. 232-233.

17. The Bajío area, in general, seems to have been more highly developed industrially than the regions farther north. San Miguel de Allende had a thriving textile industry compared to the dearth of looms—even in a cottage industry—in Durango, Zacatecas, and parts of Coahuila (Wolf, pp. 184 and 189; Brading, p. 18).

18. Ramos Arizpe, pp. 19-20 and 22-23.

19. Boyd, pp. 68-69.

20. West, p. 128, footnote 21.

21. Ramos Arizpe, pp. 40-41.

22. Mena, pp. 388-389; Berlant and Kahlenberg, p. 70.

23. Jenkins, pp. 44-45.

24. Wheat (manuscript in preparation), p. 11.

25. Mena, p. 382.

26. Spillman, p. 16.

27. Wheat, *Papers*, pp. 201 and 204.

28. *Ibid.*, p. 211.

29. Kahlenberg and Berlant, p. 13.

30. Wheat, *Papers*, pp. 215 and 218; Berlant and Kahlenberg, p. 131.

31. Wheat, *Ibid.*, p. 218.

32. Gregg, p. 148.

33. Fontana *et al.*, pp. 25, 31-43, 46, and 61-71.

34. Wheat (personal communication).

35. Carrera Stampa, pp. 322-323.

4. Julio Michaud y Thomas, *Los Poblanos* (detail), 1830s, lithograph.

The Saltillo Sarape: Style

The purpose of this exhibition and catalogue is to present to the viewer and reader one of the great achievements in the history of textile arts, the Saltillo sarape. Several examples of Rio Grande and Navajo weaving, as well as of post-classic Mexican sarapes, have been included in the exhibition. This selection is for the express purpose of showing the far-reaching influence of the Saltillo design and of providing a perspective on the evolution of northern Mexican weaving into the twentieth century. It is, however, the classic Saltillo sarape of the eighteenth and first half of the nineteenth century which remains the focal point of this exhibition.

The classic Saltillo sarape is truly one of the world's remarkable textile achievements. In comparison, it equals or surpasses any of the world's great flatweave textiles. In terms of technical excellence it rivals the master weavings of ancient Peru. The elaborate complexity of its design is equal to that of the great Senna *kelims* of Persia. The richness and harmony of its colors are equal to those of the best Caucasian *kelims*. Here comparisons end. The aesthetic expression of the Saltillo sarape is unique, incomparable.

Part of the uniqueness of Saltillo aesthetics is the intensity of its visual impact. All elements of its composition combine to create a three-dimensional effect. The subtle color changes in the border designs give the illusion of a twisting, spiraling motion. The design of the field in some examples seems to undulate. In other examples it simply gives an illusion of depth above which the border and center seem to float. The center has a dynamic all its own. The concentric serrated diamond center appears to shimmer and pulsate almost as if it were trying to escape its confines. The round center, in contrast, seems serene. It often creates the illusion of being a window giving one a view into distant space. The combination of motion, space and depth of the separate components merges to create in the classic Saltillo sarape a visual statement of startling power.

There is a surprising lack of historical data concerning the various styles and design characteristics of these extraordinary textiles of northern Mexico. Their evolution and even the precise place of their origin remain obscure. The answers to many of these questions may never be fully known. However, through analysis of the sarapes themselves certain observations and evaluations can be made.

The three basic components of the Saltillo design structure are the outside or framing border, the field, and the center. The center is the dominant feature of the sarape. This composition, so distinctive of the Saltillo, is not found in any other weaving tradition of the western hemisphere, excepting those influenced by Saltillo designs.

There are two obvious design variations which appear in the center element of the Saltillo sarape. They are the serrated concentric diamond center and the scalloped round center. These two very different treatments have been considered by some earlier writers to be the distinguishing characteristic between the sarapes of Saltillo and of San Miguel de Allende.

The concentric diamond center supposedly indicates a Saltillo sarape and the round center, a sarape from San Miguel de Allende. This has been a point of some controversy; the information available is quite inconclusive. It seems more probable that the round center is a reflection of Chinese influence on colonial Mexican aesthetics. Two and a half centuries of trade between Mexico and the Orient had a profound effect on all forms of Mexican art.

Another design variation which occurs in the center element of some Saltillo sarapes is the aggregate diamond center. This center almost always appears in sarapes of small size, coarse weave, simplified design and analine dyes. It seems obvious then that the aggregate diamond center is a later development and not characteristic of the classic Saltillo sarape.

After examination of the next component, the field of the sarape, it becomes apparent that there are four distinct styles which predominate. The four styles are the vertical mosaic, the diagonal grid, the spot repeat, and the plain field. The first of these, the vertical mosaic field, is perhaps the earliest style. It seems to have been in use throughout the classic period and prevailed in simplified form up to the early 1900's. It is the style most widely associated with the Saltillo sarape. There are a number of variations which take place in this treatment of the field, all of them worked on a vertical axis. The most common variation is composed of narrow stripes running the length of the sarape, usually in alternating colors of red, dark purple, and green or blue. Separating the stripes of color are small white diamond shapes. Down the center of each colored stripe there is a zigzag line formed by contiguous, diagonal parallelograms of alternating colors.

The diagonal grid field, although not as common as the vertical mosaic, is another variation found in many classic Saltillos. It is formed by small, feathered design elements in diagonal rows of alternating colors. This field was frequently employed in sarapes using only colors of indigo blue and ivory.

The spot repeat probably evolved from the diagonal grid field, and first appeared in the late eighteenth century. It is also worked on a diagonal axis. The spot repeat is not as complex as the feathered design element of the diagonal grid. It became more prevalent in the late classic period, the second quarter of the nineteenth century. Sarapes of this late classic period tended to become simpler in the treatment of their design elements. This tendency is indicative of the growing commercial demands for Saltillos and of the weavers' need to be able to produce sarapes more quickly.

The last style to consider is the plain field. This style is the least common, and only appears in Saltillos of the late classic period. The entire field was woven of one solid color, usually natural white or brown. It was the least demanding of all the field styles as no color changes were required of the weaver. This simplification of design was another manifestation of increasing commercialism and the need to expedite production of the Saltillo. It should be emphasized however that all Saltillos of the classic period reflect integrity of design, color and proportion. Saltillos of the late classic period are also master works of textile art.

The final element of the Saltillo composition is the border. The border of the sarape functions much as does the frame of a painting. It embellishes as well as defines the artistic statement. There is a wide range of border treatment. One of the more common variations consists of criss-crossing diagonal lines which create a lattice effect. Another popular treatment involves repeating parallel diagonal lines formed of small, contiguous design elements. A third variation, frequently seen, is composed of small design elements arranged in a diamond pattern. The zigzag border is a fourth variation. While other border treatments occur, these are the styles that predominate during the classic era.

Besides composition of design, there are two other factors essential to the aesthetics of the Saltillo sarape. These are weaving skill and the use of color. To create the finely-detailed, complex design structure of a Saltillo required a complete mastery of weaving technology, including spinning. In most sarapes the weft count exceeds 70 per inch, and it is not unusual to find weft counts in excess of 100 per inch.

Color is as important as weave and design are. The natural dyes used in classic Saltillos produced superb colors: deep, rich and lustrous. It is the juxtaposition of these colors that creates the prismatic shimmering of the diamond centers. The spiraling motion of the border and the undulation of the field are the result of subtle variegation of color. The illusion of three-dimensional space is effected by contrasting areas of varying color density, as well as areas of design. Always the quality of color is excellent and the combinations, harmonious.

The classic Saltillo is a total aesthetic statement, reflecting intelligence and sensitivity in every aspect of weave, design and color. The timeless beauty of these superb textiles is lasting testimony to the genius of the anonymous weavers of old Saltillo.

JAMES JETER

Selected Bibliography

Aveleyra A de A, Luis *et al.*, "Cueva de la Candelaria: Vol. I." *Memorias del Instituto Nacional de Antropología e Historia: V.* Instituto Nacional de Antropología e Historia, Mexico. 1956.

Berlant, Anthony and Mary Hunt Kahlenberg, *Walk in Beauty: The Navajo and Their Blankets.* New York Graphic Society (Little, Brown and Company). Boston. 1977.

Bolton, Herbert Eugene, *Texas in the Middle Eighteenth Century: Studies in Spanish Colonial History and Administration, University of California Publications in History,* III. Berkeley. 1915.

Boyd, E., *Popular Arts of Spanish New Mexico.* Museum of New Mexico Press. Santa Fe. 1974.

Brading, D. A., *Miners and Merchants in Bourbon Mexico: 1763-1810, Cambridge Latin American Studies Series,* X. Cambridge University Press. 1971.

Carrera Stampa, Manuel, "Las Ferias novohispanas," *Historia Mexicana,* vol. II, no. 7.

Chavez Orozco, Luís, *Páginas de historia económica de México,* Oficina de Máquinas de la Secretaria de Educación Pública. Mexico. n.d.

Chevalier, François, *Land and Society in Colonial Mexico: The Great Hacienda.* Trans. Alvin Eustis; Ed. Lesley Byrd Simpson. University of California Press. 1963.

Cue Canovas, Augustín, *Historia social y económica de México (1521-1854).* Editorial Trillas. Mexico. 1973.

Díaz del Castillo, Bernal, *True History of the Conquest of New Spain.* Trans. J. M. Cohen. Penguin Books. London. 1963.

Florescano, Enrique and Isabel Gil, (Comps.), *Descripciones económicas generales de Nueva España, 1784-1817, Fuentes para la historia económica de México,* no. 1. Instituto Nacional de Antropología e Historia, Seminario de Historia Económica. Mexico. 1973.

Fontana, Bernard L. *et al., The Other Southwest: Indian Arts and Crafts of Northwestern Mexico.* The Heard Museum. Phoenix. 1977 (exhibition catalogue).

Gibson, Charles, *Tlaxcala in the Sixteenth Century.* Stanford University Press. Stanford. 1967 (f.p. 1952).

Gregg, Josiah, *Commerce of the Prairies.* Ed. Max L. Moorhead. University of Oklahoma Press. Norman. 1954.

Heers, Jacques, "La Búsqueda de colorantes," *Historia Mexicana.* vol. XI. no. 41.

Humboldt, Alexander von, *Political Essay on the Kingdom of New Spain.* Trans. John Black; Ed. Mary Maples Dunn. Alfred A. Knopf. New York. 1972 (abridged edition; f.p. Paris, 1811-1812).

Jenkins, Katharine Drew, *An Analysis of the Saltillo Style in Mexican Sarapes.* Unpublished master's thesis. University of California. Berkeley. 1951.

Johnson, Irmgard Weitlaner, *Los Textiles de la Cueva de la Candelaria, Coahuila.* Instituto Nacional de Antropología e Historia. Mexico. 1977.

Kagan, Samuel, *Penal Servitude in New Spain: The Colonial Textile Industry.* Unpublished doctoral dissertation. City University of New York. 1976.

Kahlenberg, Mary Hunt and Anthony Berlant, *The Navajo Blanket.* Praeger Publishers (in association with the Los Angeles County Museum of Art). New York and Los Angeles. 1972 (exhibition catalogue).

Lacas, M. M., "A Social Welfare Organizer in 16th Century New Spain," *The Americas,* vol. XIV. 1948.

Marín de Paalen, Isabel, *Historia general del arte mexicano, etno-artesanías y arte popular.* Editorial Hermes, S.A. Mexico-Buenos Aires. 1974.

Mena, Ramón, "El Zarape," *Anales del Museo Nacional de Arqueología, Historia y Etnografía,* Tomo III (cuarta época). Mexico. 1925.

Mera, H. P., *Pueblo Indian Embroidery, Memoirs of the Laboratory of Anthropology*, IV. Santa Fe. 1943.

Powell, Philip Wayne, *Soldiers, Indians, and Silver: The Northward Advance of New Spain, 1550-1600*. University of California Press. Berkeley and Los Angeles. 1952.

—————————, *Mexico's Miguel Caldera: The Taming of America's First Frontier, 1548-1597*. University of Arizona Press. Tucson. 1977.

Ramos de Arizpe, Miguel, *Report that Dr. Miguel de Arizpe, Priest of Borbon, and Deputy in the Present General and Special Cortes of Spain for the Province of Coahuila, one of the four Eastern Interior Provinces of the Kingdom of Mexico, Presents to the August Congress on the Natural, Political and Civil Condition of the Provinces of Coahuila, Nuevo Leon, Nuevo Santander and Texas of the Four Eastern Interior Provinces of the Kingdom of Mexico*. Translated and annotated by Nettie Lee Benson. *The University of Texas Institute of Latin-American Studies*, XI. Greenwood Press, Pubs. New York. 1969.

Simpson, Lesley Byrd, *Many Mexicos*. G. P. Putnam's Sons. New York. 1946 (revised edition; f.p. 1941).

Smith, C. E. and R. S. MacNeish, "Antiquity of Polyploid Cotton," *Science*, vol. 143. 1964.

Spillman, Trish, "New Life for an Historic Craft: Rio Grande Weaving and Dyeing Workshop," *El Palacio*, vol. 83. no. 1. 1977.

Ure, Lavelle, "Mexican Textile Technology in the Sixteenth Century." Unpublished ms.

West, Robert C., *The Economic Structure of the Mining Community in Northern New Spain: The Parral Mining District*. Doctoral dissertation. University of California. Berkeley. 1946.

Wheat, Joe Ben, "Spanish-American and Navajo Weaving, 1600 to Now," *Papers of the Archaeological Society of New Mexico*, vol. III. 1976.

—————————, "Saltillo Sarapes." Unpublished ms.

Wolf, Eric R., "The Mexican Bajío in the Eighteenth Century: An Analysis of Cultural Integration," *Synoptic Studies of Mexican Culture*. Middle American Research Institute. Tulane University. New Orleans. 1957.

CATALOGUE

(entries prepared by James Jeter)

I

Classic Saltillo Sarape
First half eighteenth century
New World Arts Collection

Design Characteristics:

       Center — concentric diamond
       Field   — vertical mosaic
       Border — diagonal repeat

Length: 79 inches
Width: 54 inches
Weft: Wool, 66 per inch
Warp: Cotton, 17 per inch

Colors:	Dyes:
Dark purple	Cochineal and indigo
Purple	Cochineal and indigo
Dark red	Cochineal
Red	Cochineal
Pink	Cochineal
Green-yellow	Vegetal
Yellow	Sacatlascal (?)
Pale blue	Indigo
Blue	Indigo
Light red-brown	Wood (Brazil)
Dark brown	Natural wool
Green-brown	Natural wool
Orange	Vegetal
Ivory	Natural wool

    A rare and unusual Saltillo sarape, it is one of the earliest known surviving examples. Despite the large number of colors, the effect is one of a somber, almost brooding presence, as if it were the possessor of some forgotten archaic wisdom.

II

Classic Saltillo Sarape
Last half eighteenth century
New World Arts Collection

Design Characteristics:

    Center — concentric diamond
    Field   — vertical mosaic
    Border — lattice

Length: 99 inches
Width: 56 inches
Weft: Wool, 102 per inch
Warp: Cotton, 24 per inch

Colors: Dyes:

Colors	Dyes
Dark purple	Cochineal
Red	Cochineal
Pink	Cochineal
Blue	Indigo
Green	Vegetal
Yellow	Sacatlascal (?)
Ivory	Natural wool

This is one of the great Saltillo sarapes. It combines all the qualities — fineness of weave, color and design — that make the classic Saltillo such a magnificent textile. The center of this sarape is the ultimate in sophistication of design and beauty of color. This sarape exemplifies the pinnacle of Saltillo weaving.

III

Classic Saltillo Sarape
Last half eighteenth century
New World Arts Collection

Design Characteristics:

       Center — scalloped circle
       Field   — vertical mosaic
       Border — diamond pattern

Length: 94 inches
Width: 65 inches
Weft: Wool, 120 per inch
Warp: Cotton, 27 per inch

Colors:	Dyes:
Dark blue	Indigo
Blue	Indigo
Golden-brown	Wood (Brazil)
Ivory	Natural wool

This is another of the truly great Saltillos. Every aspect of weave and design reflects exceptional intelligence and sensitivity. This magnificent textile creates an effect of controlled excitement.

IV

Classic Saltillo Sarape
Last half eighteenth century
New World Arts Collection

Design Characteristics:

       Center — concentric diamond
       Field   — vertical mosaic
       Border — lattice

Length: 98 inches
Width: 52 inches
Weft: Wool, 100 per inch
Warp: Cotton, 20 per inch

Colors: Dyes:

       Dark purple   Cochineal
       Red   Cochineal
       Pink   Cochineal
       Blue-green   Vegetal
       Light blue   Indigo
       Yellow   Sacatlascal (?)
       White   Natural wool

This is another superb classic Saltillo. The center of this sarape has the feeling of reserved festivity underlying the power of its virtuosity.

V

Classic Saltillo Sarape
Last half eighteenth century
New World Arts Collection

Design Characteristics:

Center — concentric diamond
Field   — spot repeat
Border — zigzag

Length: 97 inches
Width: 53 inches
Weft: Wool, 106 per inch
Warp: Cotton (blue), 20 per inch

Colors: Dyes:

Purple   Cochineal
Red   Cochineal
Pink   Cochineal
Blue   Indigo
Green   Vegetal
Yellow   Sacatlascal (?)
Ivory   Natural wool

Another rare and unusual Saltillo. The extensive use of purple is quite uncommon. An interesting feature of this sarape is the use of blue-dyed warps. Whether the use of blue-dyed warps indicates a particular workshop, a place of origin distinct from Saltillo, or is just the trademark of an individual artist is unknown. It does appear in other Saltillos, all of which have a dark, usually brown field. The predominance of purple in this sarape gives it a regal quality.

VI

Classic Saltillo Sarape
Last half eighteenth century
New World Arts Collection

Design Characteristics:

        Center — concentric diamond
        Field   — vertical mosaic
        Border — diamond pattern

Length: 96 inches
Width: 48 inches
Weft: Wool, 90 per inch
Warp: Cotton, 22 per inch

Colors: Dyes:

        Dark purple   Cochineal
        Red   Cochineal
        Pink   Cochineal
        Pale blue   Indigo
        Green   Vegetal
        Yellow   Sacatlascal (?)
        Ivory   Natural wool

An interesting variation in this early sarape is the alternating colors within the small white diamonds of the field. It exemplifies the amazing attention to detail so characteristic of the fine old sarapes.

VII

Classic Saltillo Sarape
Last half eighteenth century
New World Arts Collection

Design Characteristics:

Center — concentric diamond
Field — diagonal grid
Border — zigzag

Length: 96 inches
Width: 54 inches
Weft: Wool, 80 per inch
Warp: Cotton, 19 per inch

Colors: Dyes:

Dark blue   Indigo
Blue   Indigo
Ivory   Natural wool

Saltillos using only colors of blue and white are relatively scarce. Both of the sarapes of this type in this exhibit share the same design characteristics and were probably woven by the same artist. The effect of these sarapes is one of stark, cool beauty.

VIII

Classic Saltillo Sarape
Last half eighteenth century
Santa Barbara Museum of Natural History Collection

Design Characteristics:

Center — scalloped circle
Field — diagonal grid
Border — diamond pattern

Length: 94 inches
Width: 57 inches
Weft: Wool, 72 per inch
Warp: Cotton, 17 per inch

Colors: Dyes:

Dark blue   Indigo
Blue   Indigo
Golden brown   Wood (Brazil)
Ivory   Natural wool

This is another superb example of the round-center sarape, showing the Asian influence on the aesthetics of colonial Mexico.

IX

Classic Saltillo Sarape
Last quarter eighteenth century
Santa Barbara Museum of Natural History Collection

Design Characteristics:

Center — concentric diamond
Field   — spot repeat
Border — lattice

Length: 101 inches
Width: 52 inches
Weft: Wool, 74 per inch
Warp: Cotton (blue), 19 per inch

Colors: Dyes:

Dark red-brown	Cochineal
Red	Cochineal
Pink	Cochineal
Yellow	Sacatlascal (?)
Green	Vegetal
Blue	Indigo
Ivory	Natural wool

This is another of the blue-warp Saltillos. The center of this sarape is especially beautiful. The design and colors are in perfect balance.

X

Classic Saltillo Sarape
Last half eighteenth century
New World Arts Collection

Design Characteristics:

      Center — concentric diamond
      Field   — diagonal grid
      Border — zigzag

Length: 101 inches
Width: 54 inches
Weft: Wool, 80 per inch
Warp: Cotton, 18 per inch

Colors:	Dyes:
Dark blue	Indigo
Blue	Indigo
Ivory	Natural wool

    This blue and white Saltillo, while very similar to the other, shows less contrast between the blues and has a center of greater density.

XI

Classic Saltillo Sarape
Last quarter eighteenth century
New World Arts Collection

Design Characteristics:

      Center — concentric diamond
      Field   — vertical mosaic
      Border — lattice

Length: 97 inches
Width: 48 inches
Weft: Wool, 80 per inch
Warp: Cotton, 17 per inch

Colors:	Dyes:
Red	Cochineal
Pink	Cochineal
Green	Vegetal
Blue	Indigo
Dark purple	Cochineal
Yellow	Vegetal
Ivory	Natural wool

This classic Saltillo has a center of tremendous intensity. It seems to burn with internal energy.

XII

Classic Saltillo Sarape
End of eighteenth century
Michael Caden Collection

Design Characteristics:

      Center — concentric diamond
      Field   — vertical mosaic
      Border — diagonal repeat

Length: 92 inches
Width: 51 inches
Weft: Wool, 64 per inch
Warp: Cotton, 18 per inch

Colors:	Dyes:
Black	Wood (Brazil)
Red	Cochineal
Pink	Cochineal
Blue	Indigo
Blue-green	Vegetal
Yellow	Sacatlascal (?)
Ivory	Natural wool

    This fine old Saltillo has great balance of design and color. The use of black is seldom seen. The border is a particularly beautiful version of the diagonal repeat style.

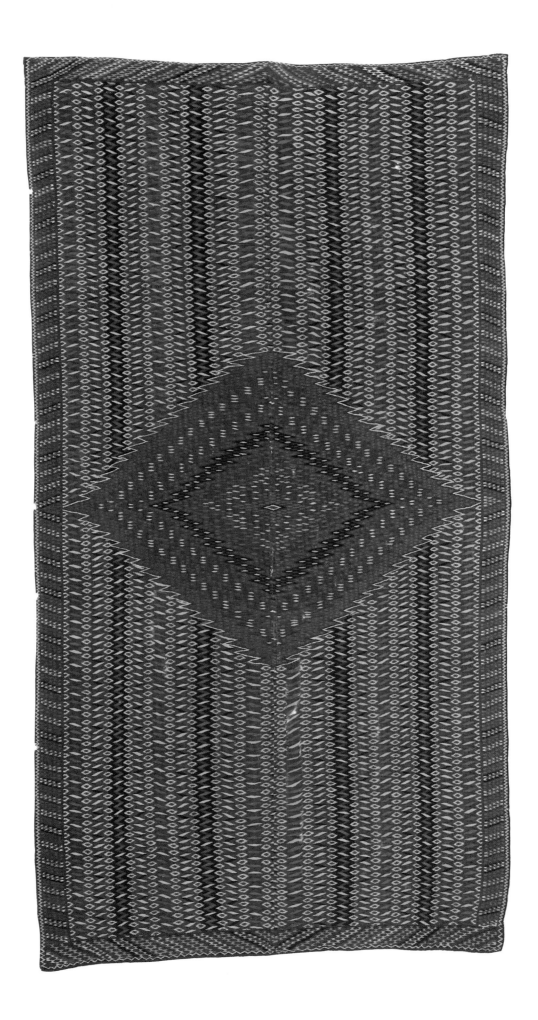

XIII

Classic Saltillo Sarape
First quarter nineteenth century
New World Arts Collection

Design Characteristics:

    Center — spot repeat
    Field   — scalloped circle
    Border — diagonal repeat

Length: 94 inches
Width: 55 inches
Weft: Wool, 66 per inch
Warp: Cotton, 22 per inch

Colors:	Dyes:
Dark blue	Indigo
Pale blue	Indigo
Gold-brown	Wood (Brazil)
Ivory	Natural wool

This sarape has a quiet, understated yet sophisticated elegance.

XIV

Classic Saltillo Sarape
First quarter nineteenth century
New World Arts Collection

Design Characteristics:

    Center — concentric diamond
    Field   — feathered spot repeat
    Border — lattice

Length: 100 inches
Width: 50 inches
Weft: Wool, 70 per inch
Warp: Cotton, 14 per inch

Colors:	Dyes:
Dark red-brown	Cochineal
Red	Cochineal
Pink	Cochineal
Yellow	Sacatlascal (?)
Green	Vegetal
Blue-green	Indigo and vegetal
Light blue	Indigo
Ivory	Natural wool

The treatment of the field in this Saltillo is unusual in its asymmetry that approaches whimsy. The overall effect of this sarape is one of simple, subdued elegance.

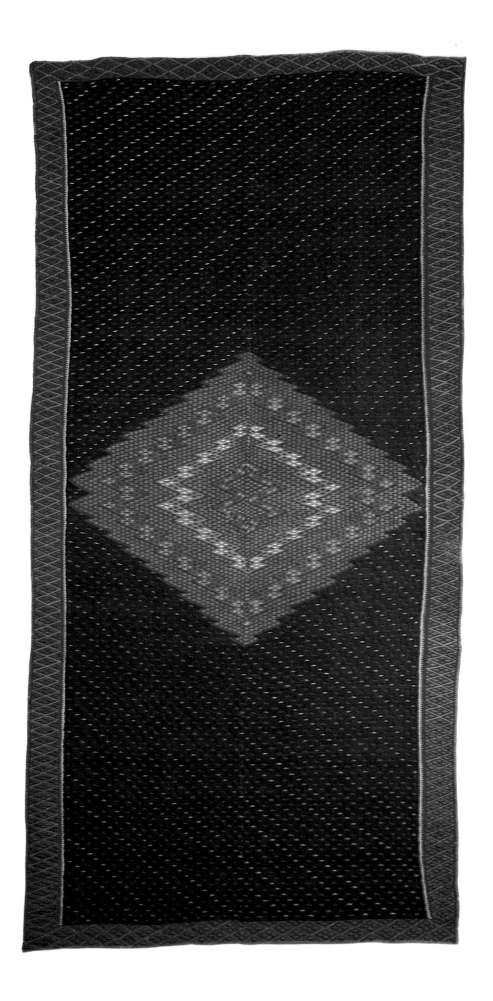

XV

Classic Saltillo Sarape
First quarter nineteenth century
New World Arts Collection

Design Characteristics:

  Center — concentric diamond
  Field — spot repeat
  Border — diamond pattern

Length: 91 inches
Width: 51 inches
Weft: Wool, 82 per inch
Warp: Cotton, 19 per inch

Colors: Dyes:

  Dark blue   Indigo
  Blue   Indigo
  Red-brown   Wood (Brazil)
  Light purple   Cochineal
  Ivory   Natural wool

The absence of red in this sarape is quite unusual. The effect is one of exquisite, almost feminine, delicacy.

XVI

Classic Saltillo Sarape
First quarter nineteenth century
New World Arts Collection

Design Characteristics:

      Center — concentric diamond
      Field   — spot repeat
      Border — zigzag

Length: 98 inches
Width: 51 inches
Weft: Wool, 62 per inch
Warp: Cotton, 17 per inch

Colors:	Dyes:
Dark purple	Cochineal
Red	Cochineal
Pink	Cochineal
Blue	Indigo
Blue-green	Indigo and vegetal
Ivory	Natural wool

A fine later classic sarape with a particularly graceful center.

XVII

Classic Saltillo Sarape
First half nineteenth century
New World Arts Collection

Design Characteristics:

       Center — concentric diamond
       Field   — plain
       Border — parallel diagonal

Length: 86 inches
Width: 43 inches
Weft: Wool, 74 per inch
Warp: Cotton, 19 per inch

Colors:	Dyes:
Red	Cochineal
Brown	Wood (Brazil)
Pink	Cochineal
Blue	Indigo
Ivory	Natural wool

This late classic Saltillo has reduced the elements of design to their simplest form. It is a beautifully refined artistic statement.

XVIII

Classic Saltillo Sarape
First half nineteenth century
Michael Caden Collection

Design Characteristics:

    Center — concentric diamond
    Field — vertical mosaic
    Border — diamond pattern

Length: 94 inches
Width: 62 inches
Weft: Wool, 52 per inch
Warp: Cotton, 14 per inch

Colors: Dyes:

    Red   Cochineal
    Pink   Cochineal
    Dark blue   Indigo
    Blue   Indigo
    Green   Vegetal
    Yellow   Vegetal
    Ivory   Natural wool

This is a late classic sarape showing a unique interpretation of the vertical mosaic field. The rosettes in the border are almost floral, an effect resulting from a subtle color change.

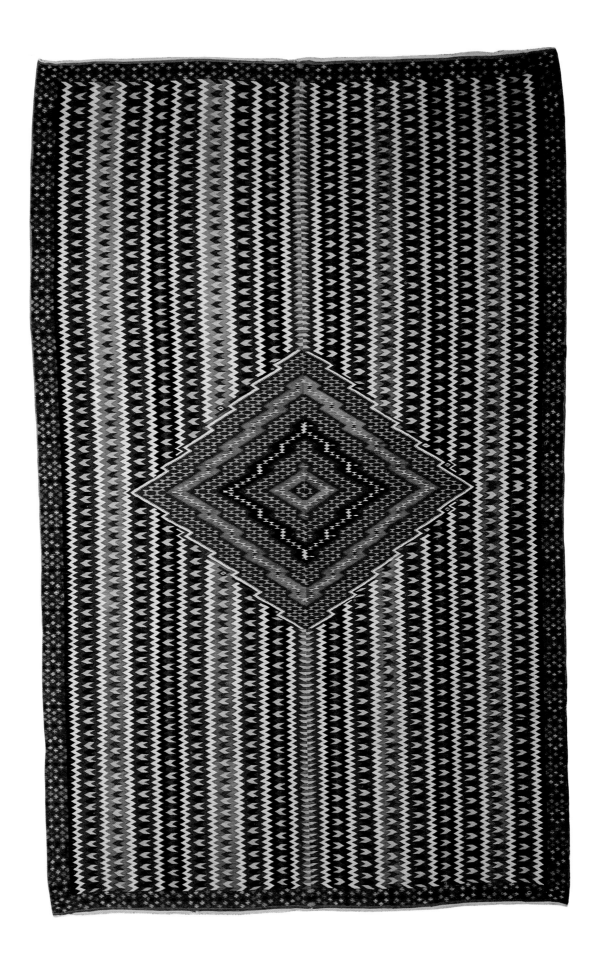

XIX

Classic Saltillo Sarape
Mid-nineteenth century
New World Arts Collection

Design Characteristics:

Center — scalloped circle
Field   — spot repeat
Border — diamond pattern

Length: 90 inches
Width: 52 inches
Weft: Wool, 50 per inch
Warp: Cotton, 10 per inch

Colors: Dyes:

Colors	Dyes
Brown-black	Natural wool
Red	Cochineal
Yellow	Palo morelete (?)
Gold-green	Vegetal
Ivory	Natural wool

This is an interesting sarape, as cochineal does not often appear in round center sarapes. Both the quality of weave and the design in the field indicate it was probably woven near the end of the classic period. The center, however, reflects a heritage of pre-Hispanic design.

XX

Saltillo Sarape
Last half nineteenth century
Michael Caden and David Hall Collection

Design Characteristics:

    Center — aggregate
    Field   — banded
    Border — banded

Length: 81 inches
Width: 42 inches
Weft: Silk (?), 94 per inch
Warp: Commercial cotton, 29 per inch

Colors:	Dyes:
Reds	Undetermined
Browns	Undetermined
Blues	Undetermined
Greens	Undetermined
Purples	Undetermined
Oranges	Undetermined
Ivory	Natural wool

    This fine sarape was woven for the wealthy *charros;* it is an aristocrat of the period. The excitement of the center is offset by the austerity of field and border.

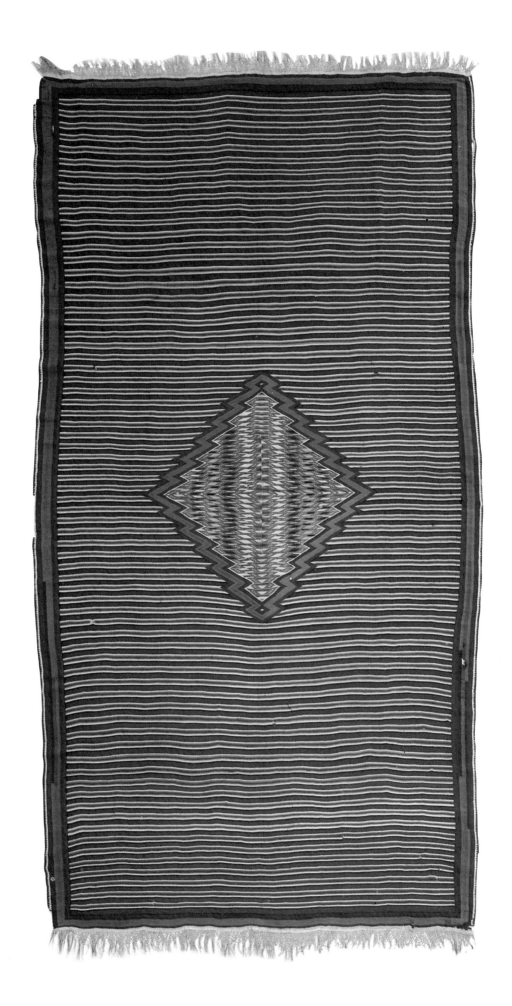

XXI

Saltillo Sarape
Last half nineteenth century
Peter Brock Collection

Design Characteristics:

      Center — aggregate diamond
      Field   — vertical mosaic
      Border — zigzag

Length: 78 inches
Width: 44 inches
Weft: Wool, 62 per inch
Warp: Cotton, 15 per inch

Colors:	Dyes:
Dark brown-black	(?)
Wine red	Cochineal
Purple	Cochineal
Blue	Indigo
Pale blue	Indigo
Pink	Cochineal
Green	Vegetal
Yellow-green	Vegetal
Yellow	Sacatlascal (?)
Ivory	Natural wool

This sarape represents "best of type" of the aggregate-diamond Saltillo that predominated during the second half of the nineteenth century. It is quite rare to find a post-classic Saltillo of this style with all natural dyes.

XXII

Saltillo Sarape
Last half nineteenth century
John Gale Collection

Design Characteristics:

Center — circular
Field — vertical mosaic
Border — late border style with banded panel on both ends

Length: 82 inches
Width: 48 inches
Weft: Wool, 50 per inch
Warp: Cotton, 15 per inch

Colors: Dyes:

Blue   Indigo
Brown   Natural wool
Beige   Natural wool
Red-brown   Wood (Brazil)
Red   Analine
Ivory   Natural wool

This post-classic sarape has an aura of quiet, self-contained power.

XXIII

Mexican Sarape
Last half nineteenth century
Peter Brock Collection

Design Characteristics:

    Center — aggregate and concentric diamond
    Field   — spot repeat and banded
    Border — none

Length: 103 inches
Width: 51 inches
Weft: Wool, 58 per inch
Warp: Cotton, 14 per inch

Colors: Dyes:

Colors	Dyes
Wine red	Cochineal
Light purple	Cochineal
Pink	Cochineal
Dark blue	Indigo
Blue	Indigo
Green	Vegetal
Green-gold	Vegetal
Yellow	Palo morelete (?)
Ivory	Natural wool

This handsome sarape, not a Saltillo, is from some weaving center further south. It shows the influence of Saltillo design in its diamond center and spot-repeat field in the central zone. A puzzling feature of this sarape is the selvage edges. They have been finished off in the traditional Navajo style. This would seem to indicate this sarape was possibly the product of a Navajo slave.

83

XXIV

Classic Saltillo Sarape
Mid-nineteenth century
New World Arts Collection

Design Characteristics:

Center — concentric diamond
Field   — spot repeat
Border — atypical

Length: 100 inches
Width: 50 inches
Weft: Wool, 64 per inch
Warp: Cotton, 16 per inch

Colors: Dyes:

Red   Cochineal
Pink   Cochineal
Green   Vegetal
Blue   Indigo
Yellow   Vegetal
Brown   Wood (Brazil)
Dark blue   Indigo
Peach   Vegetal
Ivory   Natural wool

A late classic sarape with several unusual characteristics. The absence of side borders is quite uncommon. The simplicity of the end borders is also atypical. The center is an aberrant version of the concentric diamond. The contrast of the colors is rather diffused, creating a pastel effect. It is an unusual but pleasing sarape.

XXV

Navajo Blanket
Last half nineteenth century
Peter Brock Collection

Design Characteristics:

> Horizontal panels overlaid with rows of
> contiguous diamonds interspersed with crosses.

Length: 83 inches
Width: 61 inches
Weft: Wool, 48 per inch
Warp: Wool, 15 per inch

Colors:	Dyes:
Red	Cochineal
Blue	Indigo
Green	Vegetal
Yellow	Vegetal
Ivory	Natural wool
Black	Vegetal

This is a magnificent example of classical Navajo weaving. It shows the Navajos' bold interpretation and incorporation of the Saltillo diamond into their design repertoire. The palette of this blanket with the inordinate amounts of green and yellow also indicates the impact of the Saltillo aesthetics on Navajo taste.

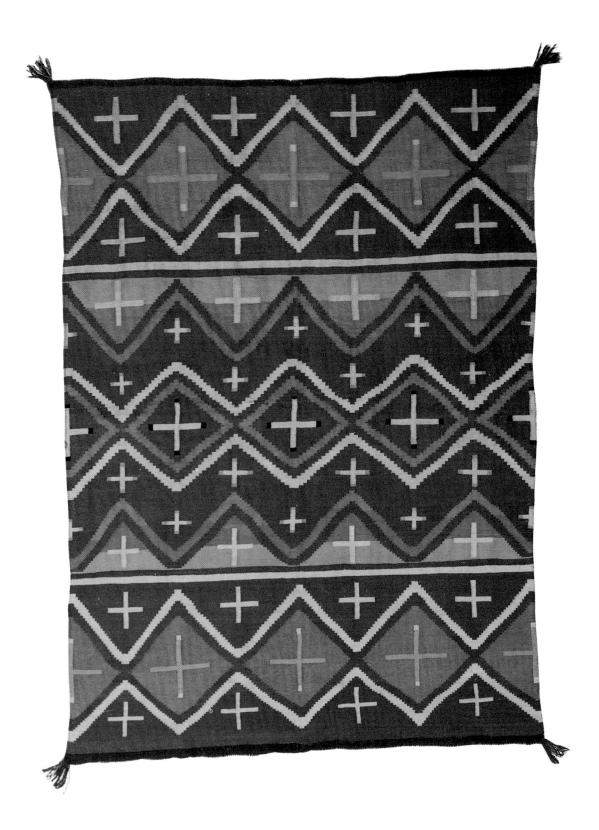

XXVI

Rio Grande Sarape
Last half nineteenth century
Peter Brock Collection

Design Characteristics:

Center — concentric diamond
Field — diagonal grid
Border — parallel diagonal

Length: 84 inches
Width: 47 inches
Weft: Wool, 44 per inch
Warp: Cotton, 10 per inch

Colors: Dyes:

Purple   Analine
Light purple   Analine
Red   Cochineal (?)
Pink   Analine
Yellow   Analine
Green   Analine
Pale green   Analine
Ivory   Natural wool

This Rio Grande sarape has taken all the components of Saltillo design and simplified and enlarged them. This interpretation of the Saltillo design is quite striking.

XXVII

Navajo Blanket
Last quarter nineteenth century
John Gale Collection

Design Characteristics:

    Overall serrated diamond pattern

Length: 74 inches
Width: 45 inches
Weft: Wool, commercial 4-ply, 38 per inch
Warp: Cotton, 10 per inch

Colors:	Dyes:
Red	Analine
Purple-gray	Analine
Pink	Analine
Dark red	Analine
Green	Analine
Black	Analine
Ivory	Natural wool

    The overall serrated diamond pattern of this Navajo "Germantown" blanket reflects the influence the Saltillo sarape had on the design of Navajo textiles throughout the second half of the nineteenth century.

XXVIII

Rio Grande Sarape
Last half nineteenth century
Michael Caden and David Hall Collection

Design Characteristics:

Center — concentric diamond
Field   — diagonal and horizontal bands
Border — sides, zigzag; ends, banded

Length: 91 inches
Width: 48 inches
Weft: Wool, 36 per inch
Warp: Cotton, 10 per inch

Colors: Dyes:

Red   Analine
Peach   Analine
Blue   Analine
Purple   Analine
Blue-green   Analine
Ivory   Natural wool

This Rio Grande sarape combines both Saltillo and Rio Grande design elements. The concentric diamond in the center reflects the Saltillo influence. The "vallero" star is a Rio Grande innovation.

XXIX

Printed Saltillo (Germany)
Last quarter nineteenth century
Wizard and Rose Collection

Design Characteristics:

      Center — aggregate diamond
      Field   — banded
      Border — interlocking diamond

Length: 83 inches
Width: 47 inches
Weft: Wool, machine woven
Warp: Cotton

Colors:	Dyes:
Reds	Analine
Oranges	Analine
Blues	Analine
Greens	Analine
Yellow	Analine
Pink	Analine
Brown	Analine
Ivory	Natural wool

    This colorful sarape was machine woven and printed in Germany in the late nineteenth century. Produced for the Mexican market, it indicates the extent of the popularity of the Saltillo sarape and that its fame had reached Europe.

XXX

Mexican Sarape (Zacatecas)
Twentieth century
Michael Caden and John Gale Collection

Design Characteristics:

    Center — oval portrait of George Washington
    Field   — banded

Length: 94 inches
Width: 44 inches
Weft: Wool and cotton or silk, 84 per inch
Warp: Cotton, 21 per inch

Colors: Dyes:

Colors	Dyes
Black	Analine
Purple	Analine
Light purple	Analine
Red	Analine
Blue	Analine
Yellows	Analine
Browns	Analine
Maroons	Analine
Pink	Analine
Ivory	Natural wool
Greens	Analine

These portrait sarapes were woven in Zacatecas and were called "Gobelinos" after the French tapestries, because of the figuration work.